Laughter for Days When You're At Your Wit's End!

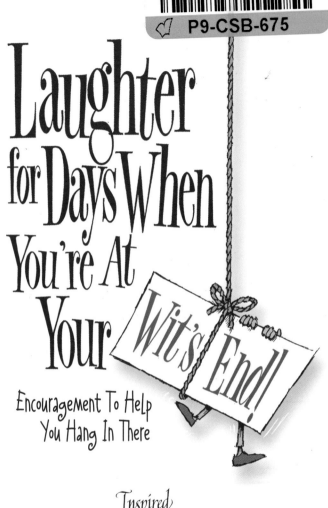

Encouragement To Help You Hang In There

Inspired by Faith

Laughter for Days When You're At Your Wit's End
ISBN 978-0-9886719-5-9

Published by Product Concept Mfg., Inc.
2175 N. Academy Circle #200, Colorado Springs, CO 80909

©2013 Product Concept Mfg., Inc. All rights reserved.

Written and Compiled by Patricia Mitchell
in association with Product Concept Mfg., Inc.

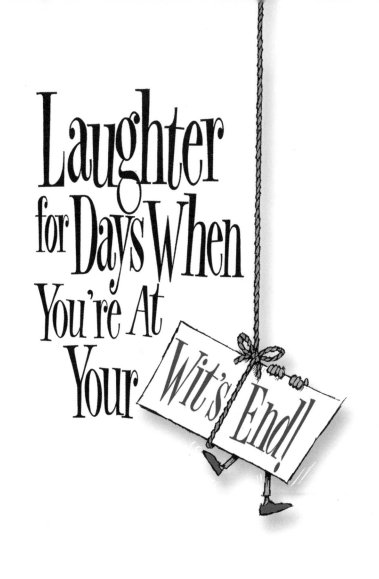

Laughter
for Days When
You're At
Your Wit's End!

Against the assault of laughter nothing can stand.

Mark Twain

Sometimes you just have to laugh!

Here's a collection of jokes, stories, one-liners, and inspiring thoughts aimed to make you smile. No matter what's going on in your day, you can jump to the section where you could use a few chuckles, or simply take your grins page by page as they come.

Sit down, relax, and take time out for Laughter now!

I Love You to Pieces, But...

Who are the people guaranteed to drive you absolutely nuts? Yep—the people you know the best and who know you the best. The people you eat with, chat with, and live with. The ones you absolutely love! And how about those eccentric relatives and oddball neighbors of yours? While we're at it, why stop with people? Why does the cat suddenly vanish whenever you call her in for the night? How come the dog needs to sniff every rock, bush, and tree whenever you're late for an appointment?

You have to wonder.

In the Neighborhood

Instant Empathy

A man was trying to cross the street in front of his house. Every time he stepped off the curb, a car came seemingly out of nowhere, barreled straight at him, and then swerved at the last minute, missing him by less than an inch. Finally, after another speeding lunge at the man, the car screeched to a halt.

Beside himself with fear and anger, the man ran to the car and pounded on the driver's window, fully expecting to see one of the neighborhood rascals at the wheel. Instead he spied a squirrel in the driver's seat. The rodent rolled down the window and glared at the man. "See?" screamed the squirrel, "now you know how I feel when you're barreling home and I'm trying to get across this stupid street!"

Getting Along...or Not!

10 Ways to Annoy Everyone You Meet

1. Drum your fingers on every surface you can find.
2. Push all the buttons before exiting the elevator.
3. Reply to every question with a question.
4. Tie jingle bells to your shoe laces.
5. Talk about yourself in third person.
6. Sprinkle every conversation with political jargon.
7. Let your turn signal blink for the whole trip.
8. Answer "How are you?" with a long, detailed description of your current physical and emotional health.
9. Emphatically emphasize the obvious—for example, add that your drive-thru order is "to-go," or announce that it's hot/cold/raining/snowing outside.
10. Break into a slow, goofy grin before replying to what other people say.

Fab Friends

New vs. Old

Over lunch, two long-time friends were talking about their husbands. "You know, the older I get, the less interest he has in me," sighed one of the women.

"Oh," her friend said with not a little satisfaction in her voice, "it's just the opposite at my house. The older I get, the more attention he pays to me!"

"Let me remind you that my husband is a new car salesman," replied the first women with equal satisfaction, "and yours is an antique dealer."

A Little Bit to Think About

A Smile Can Do That

In a rare fit of enthusiasm, a woman bought a quart of sunshine-yellow paint. It'd brighten the kitchen, she thought to herself as she pictured a freshly decorated space. That was a year ago, though, and all those months that the can had sat there in the garage, she was sure it wore a sarcastic sneer on its face. "Have you painted your kitchen yet? Huh? Huh?" it taunted as she'd slink to her car in guilty shame.

One Saturday, tired of being accused by a quart of paint, she grabbed the thing by its handle, took it to the kitchen, pried open the lid, and dipped in the brush. Little by little, stroke by stroke, the room began to glow like a fresh, warm smile. She was pleased.

When she finished, with the paint can finally empty and tossed, she stepped back to survey her work. Yes, she thought, a smile is like a coat of yellow paint. It's not any use if it's put off to another day or kept on a shelf with a lid on it. You have to get it out there. You have to spread it around. And then it's beautiful.

Home Sweet Home

Room for All

After months of searching, the Browns finally found a home large enough to accommodate their family of six. Little Rodger was especially delighted. As he was showing one of his friends around his new digs, he loudly bragged, "See? I get my own room, and so does Jill, and so does Jackie. There's even a nursery for baby Jason!" But then he lowered his voice as he and his playmate approached the door of the master bedroom. "But poor Mom and Dad," he confided, "they still have to sleep together."

Getting Along...or Not!

The frustrating thing about guys...

- When you put candles on the dinner table for a romantic atmosphere, he asks you when the power went out.
- He says, "You look great!" but you notice he hasn't taken his eyes off the TV.
- Ask him what he's thinking, and he says, "Nothing, dear." So he's been sitting there for the last two hours and not one thought has crossed his mind?
- He can locate the chips and salsa wherever they are in the kitchen, but he can't seem to find a bowl to put them in.
- He greets you with "Hey!", and that's supposed to stand for a meaningful conversation.
- He can hear what referees on the field are saying from the top bleacher, but can't hear the baby crying who's in the same room with him.

Getting Along...or Not!

The frustrating thing about gals...

- She says, "We need to talk," and then walks away. Why? When? About what?
- "Does this make me look fat?" is a question with only one right answer, so why does she ask it?
- She has to buy a gauzy, glitzy cover for every electronic device she owns. What's wrong with plain gray?
- She brings up a problem she's having, and then she gets mad as soon as you suggest a solution.
- When she says, "Excuse me?" after something you said, she's not asking you to repeat it; she's simply giving you a chance to rethink the comment.
- She tries on a pair of ten-year-old jeans and then sobs because they don't fit any more. Why not just throw them away?

Words from Wise Guys

*He who has no fools, knaves,
or beggars in his family was begot
by a flash of lightning.*

Proverb

*Why waste your money looking up your family
tree? Just go into politics and your
opponents will do it for you.*

Mark Twain

*If children grew up according to early indication,
we should have nothing but geniuses.*

Johann von Goethe

*Keep thy eyes wide open before marriage,
and half shut afterwards.*

Benjamin Franklin

It's All Relative

Our Family Tree

- There's not a family tree in existence that doesn't have several nuts and a few bad apples on it.

- The best part of any family tree is its roots.

- Just as with any healthy tree, every leaf matters.

- People trace their family trees, because not everyone's good at drawing.

- Those who forget where they came from are like trees without roots.

- Admit it—some family trees are just a few branches short.

- Some of us can't resist the temptation to decorate our family tree.

Home Sweet Home

Robert's wife was, shall we say, a casual housekeeper. One day Robert teased her by saying, "Look! The dust is so thick on the coffee table that I can write my name in it!"

She replied sweetly, "Yes, I know. That's why I married a college graduate."

●

A woman decided to clean out her attic for the first time in years. Amid the cobwebs she found a locked chest of drawers left to her by her grandmother. Curious as to what was inside, she opened the drawers and, to her astonishment, a dozen people jumped out. Come to find out, it was a missing persons' bureau.

A Little Bit to Think About

A Good Count

There's a tried-and-true way to handle anger: Count to ten before responding. And to give the old saying a modern spin: Count to ten before pressing the Send button!

In the heat of anger, what comes out of our mouths (or lands in someone's inbox) seems like the perfect retort, considering the situation. And considering our hurt, our just dues, our point of view. But even if we're on the right side of the argument, replying later rather than sooner can protect us from embarrassment, prevent our words from hurting others, stop the argument, and save a relationship.

Unless, of course, you're like the kid who comes home from school with a bloody nose, and his mother says, "Didn't I tell you to count to ten before getting in a fight?" "I did count to ten," the boy protests, "but Billy's mom told him to count to eight!"

In the Neighborhood

How Smart?

While walking their dogs, two neighbors boasted about their smart pooches. "My dog is so smart," proudly reported the first dog walker, "that he goes to the grocery store, fetches everything on my list, pays for it, and brings it right to my kitchen counter!"

"I know all about that," the second dog walker said, clearly unimpressed.

"How in the world do you know?"

"My dog, who works at the grocery store, told me."

Home Sweet Home

Birth Lessons

For school, Tommy had to write an essay about childbirth. When he got home, he asked his mother how he was born. "Well, Tommy," his mother replied, "a stork brought you." Tommy dutifully wrote down the information.

"Then how were you born?" he asked.

Mom replied, "A stork brought me to Grandma and Grandpa."

"Then how were Grandma and Grandpa born?" Tommy persisted.

"A stork brought them, too," Mom said. Tommy scribbled a few more notes before going to his room to write his essay.

The next day, he turned in a blank sheet of paper with this disclaimer attached: "Due to the fact that there hasn't been a child born into my family in three generations, I'm unable to get enough data to complete this assignment."

Fab Friends

Diet Tip

Two girlfriends were talking over coffee. The topic? Husbands. Again. "Mine is simply impossible!" said one. "He exasperates me no end, and all we do anymore is argue, argue, argue. I'm so upset that I've lost twenty pounds in three months!"

"That's awful," her friend said. "Have you been to see a marriage counselor?"

"No, not quite yet," the distraught wife replied. "I'd still like to lose another ten pounds."

Getting Along...or Not!

Sure, I'll Take Another One of Those!

John and Jennifer were guests at a lavish reception where the hosts had prepared a sumptuous buffet. Appetizers, sandwiches, hot dishes, desserts filled the table. After greeting their hosts, they took their plates and selected among the edibles before joining the other guests.

As time went on, Jennifer noticed her husband returning repeatedly to the buffet table for more food. Furious with her husband for behaving so inelegantly, she elbowed her way through the crowd to have a word with him. "You must have filled your plate half a dozen times already," she hissed. "People are going to think you're a hog!"

"No, they won't, dear," John assured her. "I've told them it's all for you!"

A Little Bit to Think About

You're Not Alone

Sometimes it's a close friend or an understanding coworker or a caring minister. Sometimes it's someone right in your own family who really knows how to listen. That's the person who's there for you when you feel you just can't cope.

When you're able to speak candidly and honestly about your problems, solutions come to the surface. First, hearing yourself speak helps you clarify the issue. Your own words serve to soothe some of the emotions and diffuse the confusion often surrounding difficult circumstances. Second, opening yourself to someone else's perspective may result in suggestions you hadn't thought of, or point you to resources you were unaware existed.

Third, you'll discover that you're not alone. Many people don't reveal their inmost hurts until they realize that someone else is going through the same or a similar situation they have faced. They can help you in real and practical ways, because they've been there. They can lead you to love, to laughter, and to hope for the future, because they've come through it. And so will you.

Home Sweet Home

Gray Hairs

As her mother combed the tangles out of her young daughter's hair, the girl stared at her mother's mostly auburn tresses. After a few minutes, the girl said, "Mommy, how come some of your hair has turned gray?"

Hoping to make this a teachable moment, the mother replied, "Well, every time you're naughty, I get stressed, and another gray hair appears."

As her mother continued to comb, the girl contemplated the matter. Then she said, "So...I'm thinking about Grandma's hair. You must have been VERY naughty."

In the Neighborhood

One Saturday, Smith called over the fence to his neighbor.
"Say, Tom, will you be using your lawn mower this afternoon?"

"I'm afraid I will," came the reply.

"Great. So can I borrow your golf clubs?"

•

Night after night, an avid birder stood in his backyard hooting like an owl. After several nights, he finally heard a reply. Overjoyed, he hooted all the more and was rewarded by more hoots in response. For the next three months, the man hooted every night, and every night he heard hoots in return.

Just when he was about to take his findings to his ornithological society, his wife met a neighbor who lived down the street. She mentioned that her husband spends nights calling to owls.
"Oh, what a coincidence," the neighbor replied. "So does mine!"

In the Neighborhood

The field across from a row of houses offered a restful scene in a rural setting. The neighbors were perplexed one evening when they compared notes and realized that another neighbor, Ernest, had spent the entire day standing in the middle of the field. Several decided to go over and ask him what he was doing.

"I'm hoping for a Nobel Prize," he answered. Seeing the puzzled looks on their faces, Ernest elaborated. "It's a prize for people out standing in their fields."

Home Sweet Home

You know you're a mom when you catch yourself saying...

- Do you honestly think you're going out of the house in that?
- When you have kids of your own, then you'll understand!
- Forget about him/her. There are other fish in the sea.
- I'm not asking you, I'm telling you!
- So if everyone else [insert activity], does that mean you do, too?
- In my day, we...
- If you fall out of that tree and break your leg, don't come running to me.
- Now don't make me stop this car!
- Bored? How in the world can you be bored?
- You didn't learn that kind of language in this house!
- Be careful what you wish for, because you just might get it.
- Just wait until your father hears about this!

   ...or anything your mother said to you!

Home Sweet Home

You know you're a dad when you catch yourself saying...

- So do you suppose money grows on trees or something?
- Go ask your mother.
- Enough is enough!
- If it's worth doing, it's worth doing right.
- Be sure you've got your emergency money and enough gas in the tank.
- I'm not talking to hear my own voice!
- Just because it's more expensive doesn't mean it's better.
- If I see you doing that one more time, I'll...
- Call, or your mother will worry.
- You've got it so easy!
- Never mind what I did when I was your age.
- What were you thinking? Or were you thinking?

    ...or anything your dad said to you!

In the Neighborhood

After a night on the town, a young fellow invited his friends in to see his new apartment. When they came to the bedroom, his friends asked about the big brass gong sitting by his bed. "That's not a gong," he said, "that's a talking alarm clock!"

"A talking alarm clock? How's it work?"

"Watch!" said the man as he picked up a hammer and gave the gong a hearty hit.

Someone on the other side of the wall screamed: "Cut it out, you jerk, it's 2 a.m.!"

●

A schnauzer and a Dalmatian were in the local Wi-Fi café and struck up a friendship. The Dalmatian said to the schnauzer, "Want to check out my website?"

"Sure," said the schnauzer. "What's the address?"

Pleased, the Dalmatian responded: "It's www.dalmatian.dot-dot-dot-dot-dot-dot..."

Home Sweet Home

Hose to Know?

A snake went to the optometrist complaining about his eyesight. "It's getting so bad," he said, "that I can't hunt anymore. I'd like a pair of glasses."

"Sure," the optometrist replied, and within the hour, he had fixed a pair of glasses for his patient. "Come back in two weeks if there's a problem," he said.

In two weeks, the snake reappeared in the optometrist's office. "Still having trouble?" the doctor asked. "Didn't the glasses help?"

"Oh, yes, the glasses are great," replied the snake. "But now I'm suffering from depression," he sighed. "I realized that for the last two years I've been living with a garden hose."

From Dawn
to Dusk

Whether we're in the workplace or out of it... spend our days earning an income or volunteering our time...digging in the garden or watching the sales...managing a home, business, or just ourselves (perhaps the most challenging task of all!), frustrations happen. We mingle with annoying neighbors, crabby coworkers, quirky teenagers, needy friends, and limelight-loving committee members.

Are they going to change? Nope. They'll continue to drive us nuts until we change—until we can look at them and realize we've got all the makings of a great comedy script every day, wherever we are, from dawn to dusk!

Workaday World

A man and a woman were on their first date trying to get to know each other. "So," she says, "I thought I heard you say you live off the spat of the land. I think you mean the fat of the land."

"No, I mean the spat of the land," he replies. "See, I'm a marriage counselor."

●

A sales rep was on his way to see a client in another city when he got stranded in a snowstorm. He emailed his boss from the airport and said that all flights out were canceled for the next two days. His boss emailed back: "Start vacation immediately."

●

At school, the teacher asked one young student to begin a sentence with "I." The student said, "I is..."

"Oh, no...always say 'I am.'"

"Okay," said the student, who dutifully started over: "I am the ninth letter of the alphabet."

A Little Bit to Think About

A Balanced Perspective

"She looks at the world through rose-colored glasses." That's often the phrase used to put down someone who sees things as better than they are and refuses to grapple with obvious problems. Yet most of us are just the opposite. We tend to see things as worse than they are and highlight only the problems we're facing. We could use a little rosy tint to our peepers!

How you look at the world around you determines what you see. Do you find only happiness because you cannot face sorrow? Do you see only sorrow because you refuse to allow happiness in your life? A healthy, balanced perspective includes calamities as well as celebrations... injustice as well as justice...wrongs as well as rights.

Every day, what you see affects your thoughts and words, actions and decisions. How you see it makes the difference between anger and laughter, inner turmoil and peace of mind.

Workaday World

You're spending too much time on the computer if...

- You've never actually met any of your friends face-to-face.
- You get up during the night to use the bathroom, and can't resist checking your email before going back to bed.
- You email yourself notes instead of writing them on a piece of paper.
- You enter an elevator and double-click the button for the floor you want.
- Your website is more popular than you are.
- You not only know what RAM is, you know how much of it your computer has.
- You frequently byte off more than you can view.
- You refer to breakfast, lunch, and dinner as breaks to upload.
- The optician looks into your eyes and sees a screen saver.
- You've forgotten what real paper feels like.

All in a Day

A Bargain Price?

Tom, a noted cheapskate, took the lowest bid he received for the job of painting the porch. When he told his wife that a guy would come around the next day and do the work for $35, she was incredulous. "What do you mean $35?" she said. "The porch goes across the whole front of our house, and the paint itself is going to cost more than $35!" But Tom wouldn't budge.

The next day, a fellow sauntered into the yard, a can of paint in one hand and a brush in the other. After an hour, the couple heard him shout from the porch: "All done!"

"How in the world could he be finished in such a short time?" the wife exclaimed. Even Tom had to wonder. As he stepped outside, he found out.

"Easy job," the painter announced, "but let me tell you something, it's a not a porch, it's a Ferrari."

Words from Wise Guys

*It is one of the most beautiful compensations of life,
that no man can sincerely try to help
another without helping himself.*

Ralph Waldo Emerson

*You are not here merely to make a living.
You are here in order to enable the world to live more
amply, with greater vision, with
a finer spirit of hope and achievement.
You are here to enrich the world.*

Woodrow Wilson

*Life is short, and we do not have much time to gladden
the hearts of those who travel with us, so be quick to
love and make haste to be kind.*

Henri-Frédéric Amiel

Volunteering Pays

- There's no "I" in team, but there is a "U" in volunteer.
- Remember: Noah's ark was put together by volunteers. The Titanic was built by professionals.
- If someone needs a smile, offer one of yours.
- We can't always have happiness, but we can always give happiness.
- Being good is an empty claim without doing good attached to it.
- He gives double who gives unasked.
- Most people talk about the needs of society. Volunteers do something about them.
- An ounce of help is better than a pound of pity.
- We keep only what we give away.

A Little Bit to Think About

Loving What You Do

Not all of us can spend our days doing exactly what we want to do. Duty calls! We have responsibilities, and these responsibilities often take us away from something we might find more pleasing or more fun. For most of us, responsibilities—like caring for dependents, earning a living, helping others—take up the better part of our days, leaving us scant time left to indulge in personal projects.

At the same time, however, we can still love what we do. Every morning, we can remind ourselves that we're blessed with a purpose, we're needed by others, and we're fulfilling our current obligations to the best of our abilities. Now there's something to love already! But, as they say on infomercials, there's more.

There are things you do that bring you a sense of pleasure, for sure. What are they? Perhaps it's the satisfaction of serving a favorite meal, of treating others kindly, of going the extra mile for someone, of putting in a good day's work. Sometimes it's things like these that bring more joy than any other pleasure could offer.

Workaday World

A group of employees who lived in the same part of town decided to save gas by carpooling to work. They drew straws to determine who would drive first, and Clark got the nod. On Monday morning, he showed up at each house right on time. The carpool was off to a great start until he got on the highway. There he put the pedal to the metal and began weaving around cars and across lanes at breakneck speed.

Finally one woman in the back seat had the courage to speak up. "Clark, can you slow down? You're scaring me half to death!"

"Don't be scared," he yelled. "Do what I do—shut your eyes!"

Getting Along…or Not!

Ten Ways to Irritate Coworkers

1. Reheat garlic pizza in the office microwave.
2. Use an outside voice inside, especially when discussing an adorable granddaughter's latest clever comments.
3. Agree with the boss on everything. Everything! Even if he says it's raining outside and you're looking out the window to a bright, clear, cloudless sky.
4. In group meetings, always ask for explanations, even if instructions are clear.
5. Sneak up behind people and read over their shoulder for several minutes before clearing your throat to let them know you're there.
6. Set your cell phone ringtone to an obnoxious jingle and let it ring for several seconds before answering it.
7. At least once a month, go around to coworkers collecting for charities and fundraisers.
8. Fill in everyone on every detail of your life, past and present.
9. Cough. Smack bubble gum. Hum. Sigh. Clear your throat. Repeat dozens of times throughout the day.
10. Forward dozens of cute kitten and puppy emails and videos to your coworkers' inboxes every day.

Workaday World

Payday

The owner of the company and one of his managers left the office fifteen minutes before quitting time and saw a fellow lounging by the door and gazing at the scenery. "Just how much are you getting paid a week, young man?" he demanded.

"I make $300," the guy replied.

The boss took out his wallet and peeled off three one-hundred dollar bills. "Here!" he said angrily. "Take these and don't bother to come back!"

As they walked to the parking lot, the owner turned to the manager and said, "Just who was that bum?"

"Oh, he doesn't work here. He's just waiting for his girlfriend."

It's About Time

The new hire shows up late for her shift. Her boss looks at his watch and yells, "You should've been here at 8:30 sharp!"

"Why?" she asks innocently. "What happened at 8:30?"

•

The boss scheduled a mandatory meeting for all employees each Friday precisely at 4:30 p.m. One day a staffer worked up the courage to ask him why he always chose Friday afternoons for important meetings. The exec replied, "Because that's the only time I can be sure no one's going to spend time arguing with what I'm saying."

It's About Time

Look at the Clocks

One morning, a man arrived at the commuter train depot, looked up at the station's clock, which said eight twenty-five. Since he had five minutes to spare before his train was due, he ducked into the depot, bought a cup of coffee, and stepped back out to the platform only to see his train pulling out of the station.

The man looked up at the station's platform clock and realized it said eight thirty-five. He said to the station master, "Do you realize your clocks don't agree?"

"Of course they don't," the station master replied. "What's the point of having two clocks if they both say the same thing?"

Words from Wise Guys

Gladly accept the gifts of the present hour.

Horace

Light tomorrow with today.

Elizabeth Barrett Browning

*Write it on your heart that every day
is the best day in the year.*

Ralph Waldo Emerson

Make use of time, let not advantage slip.

William Shakespeare

*That man is happiest who lives from day
to day and asks no more, garnering
the simple goodness of life.*

Euripides

Finding the Joy

36 Ways to Take a Break

Take a break from the daily grind! It doesn't require a month-long stay in a luxury hotel (although if that's in the offing, go for it!). Sometimes a little time out works wonders to rest, renew, and rejuvenate.

1. Listen to the birds sing and notice the trees and flowers.
2. See fantastical animals in cloud formations.
3. Lounge in a bubble bath.
4. Look up something you've always wondered about.
5. Read a captivating novel.
6. Ponder a passage from Scripture or a meaningful quote.
7. Write a poem.
8. Concentrate on the moment.
9. Stretch.
10. Listen to soothing music.
11. Go for a massage.
12. Sip a cup of coffee, tea, or hot chocolate.

Finding the Joy

13. Take a nap.
14. Breathe deeply.
15. Daydream.
16. Read a joke and giggle.
17. Stroke a cat; walk a dog.
18. Savor an exotic fragrance.
19. Sit alone in a quiet place.
20. Pray.
21. Remember the big picture.
22. Close your eyes.
23. Clear up clutter.
24. Recall happy memories.

Finding the Joy

25. Forgive others.
26. Forgive yourself.
27. Make small but important changes.
28. Do a random act of kindness.
29. Get enough sleep.
30. Try something different.
31. Be open to serendipity.
32. Eat healthy.
33. Love others.
34. Love you.
35. Count your blessings.
36. Expect the best.

A Little Bit to Think About

On the Lookout

"Look for trouble, and you're sure to find it," the saying goes. How true!

Look for trouble in the world, and you're sure to find it. Everything that's wrong makes the headlines! Look for trouble with people, and their faults suddenly take front and center place in your mind every time you see a face. Look for trouble with yourself, and you will meet a host of inner drama queens ready to whine and wail about all your weaknesses and short-comings. Bored already? Good.

How about a change of scenery? "Look for goodness, and you're sure to find it." Look for goodness in the world, and you'll see more than you ever imagined. People helping people. Compassion winning over callousness, heroism over cowardice.

Shine a light on the goodness in others, and you'll delight in all the ways they add meaning, sparkle, and love to your days. Look for goodness in you—your gifts and talents, your blessings and abilities—because they're there for the finding. All you have to do is look.

Q&A Time

Q: *What did one elevator say to the other?*
A: *I think I'm coming down with something.*

Q: *Why was the electrician disqualified from the race?*
A: *Because he made a short circuit.*

Q: *What grows up while it grows down?*
A: *A baby duckling.*

Q: *What cheese is made backward?*
A: *Edam cheese.*

Q: *Do dragons sleep during the day?*
A: *So they can hunt knights.*

Fab Friends

The Company President

Two college roommates who hadn't seen each other in years met up at a class reunion. "Say," said Jen, "I hear you own your own company! That's so exciting!"

"It's a small company and not much to brag about," came the reply.

"Really?" said Jen, hardly believing her ears. "So how many people work for you?"

"Oh, about half," sighed the hapless owner.

Workaday Word

Three Wishes

Two junior managers and their boss were on their way to lunch one day when they came across a small exotic-looking lamp. The boss rubbed it and a genie appeared, offering them one wish each. The first junior manager jumped at the chance and shouted, "Genie, I want to be in the Bahamas lying on the beach!" Whoosh! He was gone.

The second junior manager grabbed the lamp and said, "I want to be in Paris sitting at a cozy café watching the world go by!" Whoosh! He too was gone.

Now it was the boss's turn. "Genie," he demanded, "I want those fools back at their desks immediately after lunch!"

Words from Wise Guys

Do not be too timid and squeamish about your actions. All life is an experiment. The more experiments you make the better. What if they are a little coarse, and you may get your coat soiled or torn? What if you do fail, and get fairly rolled in the dirt once or twice? Up again, you shall never be so afraid of a tumble.

Ralph Waldo Emerson

Live all you can; it's a mistake not to. It doesn't so much matter what you do in particular, so long as you have your life. If you haven't had that, what have you had?

Henry James

Do not worry; eat three square meals a day; say your prayers; be courteous to your creditors; keep your digestion good; exercise; go slow and easy. Maybe there are other things your special case requires to make you happy; but, my friend, these I reckon will give you a good lift.

Abraham Lincoln

All in a Day

Sleepy Cat

A woman spent most mornings working in her garden. One day a sleek, beautiful cat appeared in the yard, brushed against her, and meowed. The woman stroked the cat, and when she was ready to go in her house, the cat followed her. Once inside, the animal hopped in a cozy chair, curled up, and promptly went to sleep. A few hours later, the cat woke up and meowed to go out again, so the woman opened the door and let it out.

This routine went on for several weeks. Curious where the cat lived, the woman attached a note to its collar. The note read: "I'd like to know who owns this lovely cat. He's been spending most of the day at my house taking a nap."

The next day, the cat returned with a different note attached to his collar. The woman opened the note, which said: "He lives in a home with two toddlers and a new baby. He's trying to catch up on his sleep. Can I come over with him tomorrow?"

Workaday World

Just Doing My Job

Two friends were having lunch at a restaurant when they overheard the customer in the next booth complain to the waiter how cold it was in the dining area. "Would you please turn down the air conditioner?" the customer said.

"Certainly, sir." The server disappeared behind a screen, and after a few seconds, reappeared. But in no time, the customer called him over to his table again.

"Now I'm too hot," the customer complained. "Would you turn up the air conditioner?"

"Not a problem, sir," and the waiter ducked behind a screen for a few seconds again. This went on several more times before the customer finally paid his bill and left.

"You get the prize for patience!" the two friends exclaimed to the waiter.

"Oh, it's nothing," the waiter said. "We don't even have an air conditioner."

Finding the Joy

Nine requisites for contented living:

- Health enough to make work a pleasure.
- Wealth enough to support your needs.
- Strength to battle with difficulties and overcome them.
- Grace enough to confess our sins and forsake them.
- Patience enough to toil until some good is accomplished.
- Charity enough to see some good in your neighbor.
- Love enough to move you to be useful and helpful to others.
- Faith enough to make real the things of God.
- Hope enough to remove all anxious fears concerning the future.

Johann von Goethe

Let's Go Shopping

A woman walked in a boutique and asked if she could try on the bright red leggings in the window. "No, ma'am" the sales associate replied. "We insist that all our customers use the dressing rooms at the back of the store."

●

A line of shoppers snaked around the block in anticipation of the big sale about to take place. Five minutes before opening time, a woman walked straight to the door, pushing ahead of everyone. The people in line shouted at her and shoved her back, but she quickly turned around and elbowed her way to the front of the line. This happened three times. The last time she screamed: "Unless you let me through, I won't open the store!"

Workaday World

Words Aplenty

The president of a prestigious corporation was invited to deliver the keynote speech at an industry convention. Wanting to impress his peers, he asked his public relations manager to write him a smart, punchy, memorable speech about twenty minutes long.

After the convention, the president returned to his office and demanded to see his public relations officer pronto. When the man entered, the president bellowed: "What's the big idea of giving me an hour-long speech? Most of the audience walked out before I was halfway finished!"

The staffer was puzzled. "I wrote a twenty-minute speech," the man said, "and I gave you the two extra copies you asked for."

Workaday World

After grading tests, a teacher called two boys to her desk. "Both of you correctly answered the same number of questions, but Dick gets an A and Harry gets an F."

Immediately Harry protested. "If we got the same number right, why does he get an A and I get an F?"

"Because," the teacher explained, "where Dick wrote 'I don't know,' you wrote 'me neither.'"

●

An employee was a half-hour late coming back from his lunch break when the boss came up to him and said, "So where have you been?"

"Getting a haircut," the employee replied.

"Getting a haircut on company time?" the boss asked disbelievingly.

"Well, it grew on company time!"

"Not all of it."

"So I didn't get all of it cut off."

●

The job application form required the names of schools and when attended. One young hopeful filled in the name of his high school. For "when attended," he wrote: Monday, Tuesday, Wednesday, Thursday, Friday.

It's Only Money

Ask most of us what keeps us tossing and turning at night, and our answers will have something to do with money. Or everything to do with money! We worry about paying bills, saving enough for the future, meeting unexpected expenses, and affording our dream vacation that keeps getting put off year after year.

These chuckles won't make your bills go away or your savings account grow (sigh!), but a smile or two always has a way of letting you rest a whole lot easier!

Dollars and Nonsense

By the time we've figured out a way to make ends meet,
they've moved the ends!

●

Sure, you've got enough money to last all month—
if you don't go anywhere and don't spend anything!

●

It's true that money doesn't grow on trees.
Actually, you have to beat the bushes for it.

●

Money talks! It says Good-Bye.

●

Unfortunately, the buck stopped before it got here.

A Little Bit to Think About

Making Ends Meet

Money—there just doesn't seem to be enough of it! At least that's how it seems when unanticipated costs are added to recurring expenses, and household emergencies pile on top of daily needs. Although we know the importance of saving, we're hard pressed to make ends meet, much less put aside money for the future.

The act of saving money, however, may be more important than the amount saved. Even putting aside five dollars or so each week gets us in the habit of saving. Most of us can do this simply by forgoing a few trips to the convenience store for coffee or soda...cutting coupons for products we buy...avoiding impulse purchases like candy bars, gum, and magazines.

As we're able, we can increase the amount we save, and soon we'll have money set aside to meet those surprise expenses that have a way of finding us!

Dollars and Nonsense

You know you're in the money when...

- You haven't bothered to look at a price tag in years.
- You wouldn't consider buying a shirt without also buying trousers, belt, shoes, jewelry, and a jacket to go with it.
- You owe the IRS more money than the average person earns in a year.
- You don't have clothes you save for "good." Your entire wardrobe is good.
- You're miffed because the local gourmet grocer went out of business.
- Your hair dresser is on-call; you never have a bad hair day.
- You can retire before you're 30.
- Waiters rush to your table; your tips are legendary.

Fab Friends

Two women were talking over lunch. One proudly announces to the other, "I'm responsible for making my husband a millionaire!"

"Wow! So what was he before you married him?" asks the other.

Says the first, "A billionaire."

●

Tom was grateful that Jim was willing to lend him $100. "I'll be forever in your debt," he told his friend.

Said Jim, "Yes, that's what I'm afraid of."

●

"I'm planning on opening a joint bank account," a single woman told her friend.

"Oh?" said her friend, quite intrigued. "Is there someone special in your life?"

"No," the single woman replied, "anyone with money will do."

Words from Wise Guys

*Money will buy you a pretty good dog,
but it won't buy the wag of his tail.*

Josh Billings

*A wise man should have money in his head,
but not in his heart.*

Jonathan Swift

One must be poor to know the luxury of giving.

George Eliot

Money often costs too much.

Ralph Waldo Emerson

*Money has never made man happy,
nor will it. There is nothing in its nature
to produce happiness. The more of it one has,
the more one wants.*

Benjamin Franklin

Dollars and Nonsense

Some of us strongly believe in sharing the wealth. So we share ours with department stores, jewelry stores, spas, resorts, restaurants....

●

The big-city counterfeiter decided a small, rural town would be a good place to pass his eighteen-dollar bills. He walked into the first store he spied, picked up a couple of candy bars costing two dollars, and handed it to the clerk along with his bogus bill. The clerk looked at the bill and then looked up at him.

"Sir, would you like your change in one nine-dollar bill and one eight, or two threes and one eleven-dollar bill?"

●

"For a long time, I've been saving for a rainy day," Jones tells his buddy. "I'm proud to say that in three more months, I'll have enough to buy a well-made umbrella."

Good Idea…Not!

Did you hear the one about…

- The guy who wanted to make his fortune by digging for gold? It didn't pan out.
- The woman who couldn't get out of debt? Turns out she couldn't budge it.
- The stand-up comic who couldn't make a living? He lacked a cents of humor.
- A chance to invest in old Egyptian buildings? But it might be a pyramid scheme.
- The woman who stored all her money in the washing machine? She was accused of money laundering.
- The woodworker who was arrested? He was accused of being a chiseler.
- The wealthy baker? He knew what to do with his dough.
- The gardener who lost his life's savings? He had put it all in hedge funds.
- The author who wrote "How to Fix Airline Food at Home"? The critics said it was tasteless.
- The fellow who always lived beyond his means? He never learned to act his wage.

Q&A Time

Q: *What do you call a billionaire who never takes a shower?*

A: *Filthy rich.*

Q: *How come it's hard to live on a submarine captain's salary?*

A: *Because they can't keep their heads above water.*

Q: *How come the nickel jumped off a cliff, but the dime didn't?*

A: *The dime had more cents.*

Q: *Why did the woman put her wallet in the freezer?*

A: *Because she wanted cold, hard cash.*

Q: *What prompted the tightrope walker to see his banker?*

A: *He was concerned about his balance.*

A Little Bit to Think About

No Money Required

Simple pleasures are all around you. Look out a window and look—really look—at the trees. Better yet, go outside and run your hand along the bark, rub a leaf between two fingers, and gaze up at the broad, green canopy. Pick dandelions...smell roses...find a seashell... collect rocks. Listen to birds singing, crickets buzzing... or the deep silence of a winter landscape.

There's the simple pleasure of taking a walk around the neighborhood...going to the library and checking out a good book...returning home and settling down to read it. An hour spent to watch the clouds...to think your own thoughts...to daydream. A song to sing...a poem to write... a picture to draw...a dance to dance just for the fun of it. There are discoveries to make, mysteries to solve, beauty and splendor to take your breath away. And laughter— always laughter!

Simple pleasures are all around you...and best of all, they're free.

Dollars and Nonsense

Polly Wanna Cracker?

A man was at an auction where he spied the most gorgeous parrot he had ever seen. When the time for bidding on the bird came, the man raised his hand and bested the opening bid. Someone raised the offer, so he went higher. This kept happening, and the man, determined to get the parrot, bid way more than he had planned. Finally, however, the bird was his.

When the time came to pay the auctioneer, the man said, "This bird sure went for a lot of money. I hope he can talk."

"Oh, he can," replied the auctioneer. "Who do you think kept raising your bids?"

Ten Ways to Save Money

1. Shop garage sales and thrift stores rather than buy new.
2. Cook large quantities; freeze portions for meals later in the month.
3. Minimize fast-food meals, not only for better health, but to save money, too.
4. Keep a record of your spending; eliminate needless purchases.
5. Keep busy and active by volunteering; helping others; using free community recreation areas.
6. Give homemade gifts or personal services instead of store-bought merchandise.
7. Never window shop unless the stores are closed.
8. Cancel subscriptions you never or rarely use, and services you can provide for yourself.
9. Switch around home décor rather than buy new.
10. Plan potlucks at home with friends; meet for board games instead of a movie; gather at a public park, not an amusement park.

Dollars and Nonsense

Over lunch, two friends were talking about their daughters. "Mine is working on her Master's in philosophy," one gushed. "You know, every time she texts me, I have to run to the dictionary!"

"You're blessed," the other sighed. "Every time my daughter texts me, I have to run to the bank."

●

"My wife can't resist anything that's marked down," a man said to his buddy. "To show you what I mean, yesterday she brought home an escalator."

●

A boy walking to the football stadium swallowed a quarter. Fortunately, a man walking by saw what happened, turned the boy upside down, whacked him on the back, and the quarter popped out of his mouth.

Once on his feet, the boy said excitedly, "Hey, you must be the quarterback!"

Words from Wise Guys

While a man is contented with himself
and his own resources, all is well.

William Hazlitt

Those who are content can never be ruined.

Proverb

Money can buy the husk of many things, but not the
kernel. It brings you food but not appetite; medicine but
not health; acquaintances but not friends; servants but
not faithfulness; days of joy but not peace and happiness.

Henrik Ibsen

You never know what is enough unless
you know what is more than enough.

William Blake

Wealth consists not in having great possessions,
but in having few wants.

Epictetus

Are We
There Yet?

Whether we're planning a weekend getaway to a nearby city or packing up for a month-long jaunt halfway around the world, we're guaranteed to come back with a few good stories about what we didn't plan—a flat tire out in the middle of nowhere. A night spent at the airport sleeping on plastic chairs. A five-star hotel that didn't quite live up to its stellar rating. A week inside the beach cottage watching it rain.

Are we there yet? Sometimes it takes a little distance between us and the event before we're laughing. But in the end, admit it—it's funny!

Been There, Done That

A river tour operator boarded his group, picked up the microphone, and started to speak. After introducing himself, he thought to put his passengers at ease, as the current was quite strong that day. "Not to worry everyone," he said. "I've been up and down this river so many times that I know every sandbar every inch of the way."

At that moment, the boat struck a sandbar so hard that it threw the passengers from their seats. "See, ladies and gentlemen?" he said. "There's one of them at this very spot!"

•

The vacationers were hiking up a mountain trail where "Watch for Fallen Rocks" signs were posted at intervals. At the base of each sign, one of the hikers stopped, picked up a few rocks, and put them in his backpack. At the end of the day when they returned to camp, the rock-collecting hiker went to the ranger and emptied his backpack.

"Here are the fallen rocks," he said. "Now where's my watch?"

On the Road

Forget Something?

While on a road trip, an elderly couple stopped at a diner for lunch. After they finished eating, they paid the bill and continued their trip.

After they had gone about fifty miles, the woman reached in her purse for her glasses, but then realized she had left them on the table of the diner. Unfortunately, there was no place they could safely turn around for another twenty miles. For the whole distance, her husband grumbled about his wife's forgetfulness.

At last they reached the diner. Her husband stopped the car, and as his wife climbed out, he said, "As long as you're in there, you may as well pick up my hat and umbrella, too."

It's Time!

You know you need a vacation when...

- You start to look like your passport picture.
- When you automatically start driving to work on your days off.
- You're under the impression that your home/office/committee can't function without you.
- Every dream at night involves what you do all day.
- You try to enter your password on the microwave oven.
- You're not sure if you really want to lose that fatigued, stressed, oh-so-busy look.
- Tension lines are becoming a permanent feature of your forehead.
- You boast that you haven't taken a day off in ten years.

A Little Bit to Think About

Give Yourself a Break

We live in a fast-paced society, and few of us escape the tension and stress that go along with being active, busy, and engaged with life. Though our days are stimulating and interesting, we're often overloaded with things to do, see, and think about. Sometimes we're so overworked that we feel we can't get away, and may even feel guilty at doing so. Yet our bodies, as well as your minds, need a break!

Even a short break—say, a weekend free of home chores and work tasks, unplugged from email, voice mail, and social media—can give us the rest and replenishment we need. When we get back to our normal routine, we're better able to cope with problems, more apt to discover new ways of doing things, more productive, and equipped to enjoy the blessings of our day.

Give yourself a break—long or short, faraway on a distant shore or right in your own backyard—relax!

(Still feeling guilty? Remember: It's good for you!)

On the Road

How come we say we're "getting away from it all" when we first have to load the car with kids, pets, suitcases, pillows, blankets, games, toys, and sports equipment?

•

The couple pulled into an Orlando hotel parking lot and wondered why it was covered with snow. They later received notice that there was a minor glitch in their GPS device.

•

Remember that a journey of a thousand miles begins with an argument about how to pack the car.

•

Fred intended to take his camouflage tent to the campground, but he just couldn't find it.

We're Here!

Jack and Jill packed for a ski trip, and when they got to their cabin in the mountains, Jill noticed that Jack had brought along an enormous thermos. "What's that?" she said.

"It's a thermos," Jack replied. "The guy at the convenience store told me it's guaranteed to keep hot things hot and cold things cold."

Jill asked, "So what did you get to put in it?"

"Four cups of coffee and a couple of ice cream sandwiches."

●

A husband and wife arrived at the resort several hundred miles from their home. Suddenly the wife says, "Oh dear! I believe I forgot to turn off the oven before we left! I'm worried it might start a fire!"

"Don't worry," the husband says, "it won't start a fire."

"How can you say that?"

"Because, now that I think about it, I forgot to turn off the water in the kitchen sink."

Getting Along...or Not!

1. Never take a road trip with more kids than you have car windows.
2. Disable the sound on each video game the kids take along.
3. Make believe the car comes with an automatic massage mechanism when someone starts kicking the back of your seat.
4. Give the GPS to the kids. That way they'll never have to ask, "Are we there yet?"
5. Never stop at an historic monument or in a picturesque town under the impression that the kids will find it interesting.
6. Never put more than ten miles between food and bathroom breaks...or else.
7. Take along plenty of patience and lots of laughter!

Vacation Dollars

Travel broadens the perspective—and flattens the wallet.

•

It's easy to meet vacation expenses. Wherever you go, there they are!

•

You can still stay in some of the world's most desirable resorts for under thirty dollars a day—that is, if your day ends at 4 a.m.

•

The best place to spend a vacation is somewhere near your budget.

•

A three-part land/sea/air tour is glamorous, but the hardest part of the trip comes first—the trip to the bank.

We're Here!

The perfect place to stay is where the fish bite and the mosquitoes don't.

●

Think your ship's cabin is small? In ours, we dropped a handkerchief and it became wall-to-wall carpet!

●

Smith was offered a discount at a budget motel if he agreed to make his own bed. When he accepted the offer, the desk clerk promptly handed him a hammer, some wood, and a bag of nails.

●

We wondered why the desk clerk asked us if we had a good memory for faces—until we realized our bathroom had no mirror.

Up in the Air

Eight Clues You've Booked a Bare-Bones Airline

1. All passengers are advised that reaching their destination depends on how much they're willing to donate toward fuel.
2. The ticket agent, baggage handler, and pilot are the same person.
3. Your choice of beverages is Yes or No.
4. You notice the ground crew using dimes to check tire wear.
5. The flight attendants are wearing parachutes.
6. Your meal consists of whatever you've brought with you, or what your seatmate is generous enough to share.
7. For overseas travel, you're advised to wear a bathing suit.
8. Instead of safety instructions on the card in front of your seat, you find a selection of prayers.

A Little Bit to Think About

Not the Usual, Thank You

It's easy to get into a rut. We do the same thing each day, day in and day out. Oh, our weekend might give us a little more flexibility, but how often do we really do something different even when we can? Mostly we fall back into doing what we always do, even when we can choose something else—something we've never done before.

"Something different" doesn't have to mean "wild and crazy." Little changes in your daily routine can open your eyes to things you've never noticed before. Another route to and from work, for instance, gets you away from the scenery that's so familiar you hardly see it anymore. Instead of the usual, a restaurant you haven't been to before...a genre of music you've never really listened to...a book from a different section of the library...a movie you generally wouldn't go to see.

Rearrange your furniture. Brighten rooms with fresh flowers. Change curtains. Repaint walls. Hang new pictures. Introduce yourself to someone you don't know.

Take a break from the usual today!

We're Here!

Harry arrived at the beach, but hesitated at the shore. "Lifeguard," he called, "there aren't sharks in the water, are there?"

"No sharks," the lifeguard called back. "They don't get along with the alligators."

•

Joe and his wife had booked a cabin for the summer. When they arrived at the main office, Joe went inside to get the keys. "It's just a stone's throw from the lake," the proprietor told him.

"How will I recognize it?" Joe asked.

"Simple. It's the one with all the broken windows.

•

The hiker had a pretty close call. She went to investigate some tracks in the woods, and that's when the train almost hit her.

•

A Washington D.C. tour guide showed his group the place where George Washington is said to have thrown a dollar across the Potomac River. "That's impossible!" came a voice from the back of the group.

"You have to remember," the guide replied, "that a dollar went a lot further in those days!"

World Travelers

They Get Around

A man walked up to the airline ticket counter with a ticket to Los Angeles and three pieces of luggage. "This one," he said pointing to a blue garment bag, "I want you to send to Singapore. The brown trunk goes to London. And this one," he said as he picked up a black suitcase, "goes to Chicago."

"Sir," the ticket agent protested, "we can't do that."

"Of course you can," the passenger countered. "That's precisely what happened the last time I flew with you."

Uh-oh

Lost Something?

While on the highway, a driver was motioned over by a state trooper. When the trooper came to talk to him, he discovered that the driver was extremely distraught. "I simply can't believe this is happening!" he cried in dismay.

"Well, there's no need to get so worked up, sir," the trooper said. "All I pulled you over for is to tell you that your back lights aren't working properly."

"This is awful, awful!" the driver wailed.

"Sir, there's a garage just up the road. You can get them fixed and be out of here in a jiffy!"

"I don't care about the lights," yelled the driver. "What I want to know is, what happened to the RV I was pulling?

House Guest

City Trained

A man who had lived on a small remote island all his life decided to visit his city cousin. Everything he saw was new to him, including train tracks.

One afternoon, while sitting on the tracks, he heard a whistle, but didn't know he needed to move. The train came right at him, and fortunately he was able to leap out of the way at the last second. Later at his cousin's house he was sitting at the kitchen table when his cousin put a tea kettle on the stove. After a few minutes, the kettle started to whistle. Terrified, the man sprang to his feet, grabbed a baseball bat, and crushed the kettle to smithereens. Hearing the commotion, his cousin ran into the kitchen. "Why in the world did you do that to my tea kettle?" the cousin angrily demanded.

"I know all about these things!" his guest exclaimed. "You gotta get 'em when they're small!"

Street Smarts

Mobility? We love it! While most of us can't imagine life without our car keys, many of us take to the streets on scooters, motorcycles, bicycles, and our own two feet. In cities we'll board the bus or dash down to the subway station. Up mountains we'll ride the cable car or ski lift—and maybe hike it. Whether with the help of a gasoline engine, an electric battery, or a pair of good strong legs, we always find a way to get from Point A to Point B and back again.

So what happens when we're all out there? Sure, the traffic jams...but it's about a whole lot more. See if you can relate to these ticklers. Proceed straight ahead!

Love Those Wheels!

There's the customer who goes back to the auto dealer and says, "When I bought this car from you, you told me you'd fix anything that broke, right?"

"That's absolutely right," the dealer says. "It's guaranteed!"

"OK then," the customer says, "I need a new garage."

•

Tom asks his buddy Bill to stand in back of his car and tell him if the blinker's working. Bill obliges. Tom climbs in the driver's seat and flips the blinker switch.

"Is it working?" Tom yells.

"Yep!" says Bill. "Nope! Yep! Nope! Yep!..."

Vroom!

You know you're a car nut when...

- Your garage is bigger than your house.
- There are more car parts in the dishwasher than dishes.
- You have several shelves devoted to automobile manuals.
- You can talk about your car for over an hour without repeating yourself.
- You keep a photo of your car in your wallet.
- You know the model year of each car you own, but you're hazy about the ages of your grandchildren.
- Your idea of a great shopping experience is browsing at an auto parts store.

LOL!

A fellow decided to take the road less traveled. Now he's at the mechanic's for new shocks and a front-end alignment.

•

Dad, teaching his teenager to drive says: Remember the rules: stop on red, go on green, and slow down when I turn purple.

•

He: How often do you rotate your tires?
She: Every time I drive.

Uh-oh

After a collision on a narrow two-lane road, an officer arrived on the scene and took one of the drivers aside. "That road hog wouldn't let me have my half of the road!" exclaimed the aggravated driver. The officer then went to interview the other driver.

"He says you wouldn't let him have his half of the road," the officer explained. "Why not?"

"How could I?" the other driver protested. "The way he was driving, I had no idea which half of the road he wanted!"

●

A woman, trying to get out of a parking place, first bumped the car in front of her and then dented the car behind her. Witnessing the whole debacle, a traffic cop went up to her car and asked to see her driver's license.

"Don't be silly, officer," the woman said. "Now who do you think would ever give me a license?"

Love Those Wheels!

"I tried out one of those talking cars," Joe tells his buddy, "but I didn't like it."

"Why not?" says his friend.

"Because all it says is things like 'Your door is ajar' and 'Your gas tank is almost empty,'" the man replies. "Nothing really useful like 'There's a state trooper parked behind that bush.'"

●

A daughter goes to her dad and says, "Come and look at the car. There's water in the carburetor."

"That's silly! I doubt you even know what a carburetor is," he says. Getting up, he asks where the car is.

"In the swimming pool," the girl replies.

A Little Bit to Think About

Where Are You Going?

Imagine a traveler with a specific destination in mind. He packs a suitcase of things useful to him neither on the road nor at his endpoint. Instead of heading in the direction of his destination, he goes in the opposite direction. He takes detours that take him even further off course, and he stops in places that will only hinder him from reaching his professed destination.

We're frequently like the disorganized traveler as we go through life. We know where we'd like to be, but we're not taking any practical steps toward it. Our day-to-day choices do nothing to advance us in the direction we would like to go, and sometimes our choices even put more distance between ourselves and our objective. Is it any wonder we're far from where we set out to go?

Though you can't map out your life's journey with the same precision you might determine the best route to a neighboring town, you can know the direction you want to go, and take it. Smart preparation and good choices will help keep you on the right track.

Words from Wise Guys

*Do not go where the path may lead. Go instead where
there is no path and leave a trail.*

Ralph Waldo Emerson

*A person often meets his destiny
on the road he took to avoid it.*

Jean de La Fontaine

The only journey is the one within.

Rainer Maria Rilke

*Friends are as companions on a journey,
who ought to aid each other to persevere
in the road to a happier life.*

Pythagoras

*You traverse the world in search of happiness which is
within the reach of every man;
a contented mind confers it on all.*

Horace

Excuses, Excuses

A motorcycle cop sees a woman speeding down the highway and knitting at the same time. He grabs his bull horn and yells, "Pull over!"

"No, officer!" the woman shouts back, "It's a pair of mittens!"

●

A safety-conscious driver is pulled over for going too slow on a two-lane road. "Cars were backed up behind you," the officer says, "and no one could pass you."

"That's not true," the driver protests. "I was passed by plenty of cars going the other way!"

●

A state trooper pulls over a speeder and asks, "Didn't you see the speed limit signs posted all along the highway?"

"No, I sure didn't," the driver replies. "I was going way too fast to read those little things!"

●

A cop stops a car going 90 in a 25-mile per hour zone. "What's the matter with you?" asks the cop.

"See," the driver explains, "I lost my brakes about five miles back and I was trying to hurry home before I caused an accident!"

Fab Friends

Two friends were on a tandem bike, making their way up a steep hill. After a long and hard ascent to the top, the first guy climbed off, leaned against a fence post, and wiped the sweat from his face. "Whew!" he said, "that was harder than I thought it would be!"

The second replied, "And thank goodness I was there to keep the brakes on the whole time, or else we would have rolled downhill backward!"

•

Two friends walked into a restaurant called The Moon. They agreed that the food was wonderful, but the atmosphere was lacking.

•

A disoriented visitor to the city dashed into a cab. "Take me to the Main Street Hotel!" he demanded. The cab driver looked at him and replied, "Sir, you are at the Main Street Hotel." At that, the visitor jumped out of the cab, handed him $20, and said, "Thanks, but really, you shouldn't drive so fast through the city."

Q&A Time

Q: *What did the snail say when he hitched a ride on a turtle?*

A: *Wheeee!*

Q: *What's the hardest thing about riding a bicycle?*

A: *The pavement.*

Q: *How did the flight captain know that the aircraft had landed safely?*

A: *When the passengers stopped screaming.*

Q: *What do you call someone who misses ten car payments?*

A: *A pedestrian.*

Q: *How often do you rotate your tires?*

A: *Every time you drive.*

Love Those Wheels!

A woman asked her mechanic to put air in her car's tires. When she saw the bill, she noticed a $20 charge for the service.

"Twenty dollars!" she exclaimed. "Last year you put air in the tires for free!"

Said the cashier: "Well, that's inflation for you!"

●

He lived by the tracks, and every morning precisely at 3:00 a.m. a train rumbled by, honking its horn repeatedly. Nonetheless, the homeowner slept peacefully night after night. That is, until one day the train was canceled. At one minute past 3, the man woke with a start, sat straight up in bed, and shouted to his wife, "What was that?"

●

A man was seen driving with a penguin in the passenger seat. When an officer stopped him and asked about the penguin, the man explained that he was taking it to the zoo. With that, the officer waved him on.

The next day, the officer spotted the man again, still with the penguin in the passenger seat. "I thought you told me you were taking the penguin to the zoo!" the officer said.

"I did," the man replied. "Today I'm taking him to the shopping mall."

Bumper Stickers

Don't like my driving? Then get off the sidewalk!

We're not senior citizens—we're recycled teenagers.

The keys are on the seat next to the Doberman.

Shhhh. Don't wake the driver.

Get off the road now—student driver!

When the going gets tough, the tough go shopping.

Trust in God, but lock your car.

Stress takes its toll. Please have exact change.

LOL!

How many roads must a man go down before he admits that he's lost?

•

Even worse than raining cats and dogs is hailing taxi cabs.

•

Sign on a tow truck: Call us 24/7. We're always on our tows!"

•

He who hesitates is not only lost, but ten miles from the next exit.

•

The nervous passenger approaches the airline ticket counter. The agent asks him, "Do you have reservations?"

"You bet I have reservations!" he replies, "but I'm flying anyway."

Those Senior Moments

The Car Keys

A woman's husband was becoming concerned about his wife's frequent memory lapses. When she saw that a conference on how to improve memory was being offered at a local hotel, she decided to attend. She was pleased with the presentations, and when the conference was over, she walked out into the parking lot with newfound confidence and optimism.

Her cheerfulness quickly dissipated, however, when she realized she couldn't find her car. "Oh no!" she thought to herself, "I've done it again! I left the keys in the ignition, and now the car's been stolen!" She went back inside the hotel and alerted the security officer, who in turn notified the police.

Dreading what her husband was going to say, she called him on her cell and said...

Those Senior Moments

…"Dear, I'm afraid I must have forgotten to take the keys out of the ignition of the car, and now it's been stolen from the hotel parking lot."

Several seconds' silence on the other end of the line was abruptly broken when her husband shouted, "The car was never parked at the hotel, because I dropped you off!"

Relieved yet embarrassed, the woman said in a small voice, "Could you come and pick me up, then?"

"I'd be happy to," her husband said, "as soon as I can convince the state trooper that I haven't stolen your car!"

Just Gotta Laugh!

Here's a potpourri of stories, jokes, and anecdotes! Drawn from things that have happened—or could have happened, anyway—these tidbits of humor are here to bring a smile to your face no matter what's really happening in your day.

Along with the fun stuff, there's a little food for thought about—what else?—laughter!

Our Four-Legged Friends

The city slicker said to the rancher, "Been out for a ride this morning."

"Horseback?" said the rancher.

"Yep," replied the city slicker, "he got back about an hour before I did."

●

A little girl walked into the pet store and asked the owner if he had any sharks for sale. "Why do you want a shark?" the owner asked.

She answered: "Because my cat keeps trying to eat my goldfish, and I want to teach him a lesson."

●

Dad decides to surprise his kids with the puppy they've been begging for. He walks into the pet store and asks if they have any pups going cheap.

"Nope," says the clerk, "all ours go 'arf, arf.'"

If Something Can Go Wrong...

There's nothing else to do but laugh when...

- You were supposed to bring the baked beans to the picnic. You remembered when you found the pan of beans a week later right where you left them, in the trunk of your car.
- You're so busy that it's been a month since you've had time to vacuum the house, and out-of-town friends drop in for a surprise visit.
- You call for reservations at a popular chain restaurant for a party of twelve. After everyone's arrived, you discover that they've booked you at their other site located 50 miles away.
- You and your sister are ten years apart in age, yet people keep asking who's the oldest.
- You're hosting Thanksgiving dinner, and everything turns out great—except the turkey!

Hey, Doc!

The nurse said, "Doctor, there's an invisible man in the waiting room."

The doctor replied, "Go out and tell him that I can't see him right now."

•

The patient was telling her physician about her problems. "Whenever I touch my head, it hurts," she said, "and when I touch my chest, it hurts. When I touch my elbow, it hurts; and when I touch my knee, it hurts, too."

"Hmmm," the physician replied. "Looks as if you've got a broken finger!"

•

"I got this great new hearing aid," a guy announced to his friend. "It cost me a ton of money, but it works great."

"Really?" replied the friend. "What kind is it?"

"Twelve-thirty!"

Music to Your Ears

Grandpa bought Tommy a set of drums for his birthday. A month later, he asked Tommy how he liked them. "I love them!" reported the boy. "I've already earned $300 with them!"

"That's wonderful, Tommy," his grandfather said. "You must be really good at playing them."

"Not really," Tommy said. "It's just that Mom gives me $5 not to play them during the day, and Dad gives me $5 not to play them when he gets home at night."

●

A woman heard a knock at the door and opened it to see a man carrying a case full of tools. "I'm the piano tuner," the man said.

She said, "I didn't call a piano tuner."

"I know, but your neighbors did."

●

"My neighbors were screaming and shouting at 2 a.m. last night," Tom complained to his coworker.

"That's terrible!" the coworker sympathized. "I imagine they woke you up."

"No, actually they didn't," Tom said. "I was playing my bagpipes at the time."

A Little Bit to Think About

No-Stress Mess

Okay, so things are really a mess. Car keys locked in the car...one-hour meeting that drags on for two...sudden downpour in the middle of the annual family picnic... five snow days in a row and three bored, restless, house-bound middle-schoolers.

Preparedness, organization, and planning are all good, of course. But they have their limits, because things like car keys, meeting facilitators, the weather, and kids just won't stick with the program. They're unpredictable. So are pets, computers, bosses, and customer support. They have the ability to turn a perfectly arranged day into complete chaos. And then we stress. Really stress.

But does stress help? No. Stress simply adds another problem on top of whatever is the problem in the first place. That's why you may as well throw your hands in the air and laugh. After all, you're going to laugh later anyway, so get a jump on it: laugh sooner.

Words from Wise Guys

A good laugh is sunshine in the house.

William Makepeace Thackeray

A person without a sense of humor is like a wagon without springs–jolted by every pebble in the road.

Henry Ward Beecher

What soap is to the body, laughter is to the soul.

Proverb

Laugh and the world laughs with you.

Ella Wheeler Wilcox

LOL!

"How come you always carry three pairs of glasses?" she asks.

He replies: "One pair's for reading, one's pair's for driving, and one's pair's for looking for the other two."

●

A fellow was relating a story to his friend when he suddenly stopped talking midsentence. "What's the matter?" his friend asked. "Lost your train of thought?"

"Not entirely," the fellow replied, "but I think one of the cars might have derailed."

●

A guy walks into an ice cream parlor and asks the gal behind the counter what flavors she has today. "Chocolate, strawberry, and vanilla," she answers in a hoarse voice.

"You have laryngitis?" he says.

"No," she answers, "just chocolate, strawberry, and vanilla."

Q&A

Q: *Why should friends never do crossword puzzles together?*
A: *Because it will lead to cross words.*

Q: *Why do grizzly bears have brown coats?*
A: *Because they'd look silly in plaid.*

Q: *What's the funniest animal in the world?*
A: *A stand-up chameleon.*

Q: *Where are you guaranteed to find success before work?*
A: *In the dictionary.*

Q: *Why are leopards so easy to find?*
A: *Because they're always spotted.*

If Something Can Go Wrong...

Wake-Up Call

A husband and wife had a spat one evening that ended only after they agreed not to speak to each other. Before he went to bed, the husband, who was to leave on a business flight the next morning, left a note on his wife's pillow: "Please wake me at 5 a.m."

The next morning he woke up, looked at the clock, and saw that it was 7 a.m., too late to make his flight. He angrily sprang out of bed, ready to confront his wife with this newest infraction, when he saw this note on his pillow: "It's 5:00 a.m. Get up."

•

In a well-executed heist, a thief broke into an art collector's house and stole three priceless paintings. He successfully made it past the homeowner's sophisticated security system, out the estate's guarded gates, and into his getaway vehicle. He was caught with the paintings two miles down the road, however, because he had run out of gas. The arresting officer asked him, "How was it you could plan your crime so thoroughly, yet make such a stupid mistake as running out of fuel?"

The thief replied, "Because I had no Monet to buy Degas to make the Van Gogh."

Our Four-Legged Friends

Perfectly Qualified

A business owner put a sign in the window of his building: "Help Wanted," the sign said. "Must be computer competent and bilingual." A dog saw the sign, trotted in, looked at the receptionist, and back again at the sign, all the while wagging his tail excitedly. She got the idea, so she showed the dog to the owner's office.

The owner said to the dog, "I'm sorry, I can't hire you, because I need someone who can use the computer." Hearing that, the dog jumped up on a chair in front of the computer and proceeded to create a beautifully formatted document. Though the owner was impressed, he said to the dog, "You're really a competent dog, I can see that; but I need someone who's bilingual, too."

To that the dog replied, "Meow."

Funny Life

Have you ever wondered...

- If it's okay to order a club sandwich when you're not a member of a club?
- How snowplow drivers get to work in the morning?
- Why women's magazines contain twice as many dessert recipes as diet tips?
- If you can buy something specific in a general store?
- How you would eat if your elbows bent the other way?
- Why the clothes hanging in your closet for a few months shrink two sizes?
- If a vegetarian would eat animal crackers?
- How a "Do Not Walk on Grass" sign got to the middle of the lawn?
- How much more water the ocean would have in it if sponges didn't live there?

Hey, Doc!

The patient goes to the doctor and says, "I really need help! I can't remember anything for more than a minute!"

"Hmmm," says the doctor, "so how long has this been going on?"

"How long has what been going on?"

●

"Every time I drink coffee, doc," the patient told his optometrist, "I get this stabbing pain in my right eye. What should I do?"

"Take the spoon out of the cup before you drink the coffee," the optometrist replied.

●

"After you have your operation," the surgeon told her patient, "you'll be a new man."

"That's wonderful news!" the patient exclaimed. "And please send the bill to the old man."

LOL!

Opening Time Yet?

The librarian was sound asleep in the wee hours of the morning when the phone rang. She answered, groggy and bleary-eyed, only to hear the caller ask her what time the library would open that day. "Nine o'clock," she said angrily. "What's the big idea of waking me up so early in the morning to ask me a question like that?"

"Um, not until nine o'clock, you say?" said the caller with obvious disappointment.

"No, not until nine o'clock!" she replied. "Why do you want to get in before then?"

The caller said, "I'm not asking to get in, ma'am. I want to get out."

Daffy Definitions

Adult.................Anyone who has stopped growing up and has started growing out.

Advertising ......A TV spot that can convince us that we absolutely need what we never even knew we ever wanted.

Book.................What you read while being put on hold for your computer's tech support.

Compliment.....An applause that refreshes.

Computer.........A device guaranteed to automate and multiply errors you can't fix.

Cosmetics........Use to prevent others from reading between the lines.

Diamond...........A chunk of coal made good under pressure.

Diet ....A short period of scarcity before a sharp gain of ten pounds.

Egoist...............Someone me-deep in conversation.

Experience.......How we like to describe our mistakes.

Feedback.........What you get when the baby doesn't care for creamed spinach.

Frown...............An upside-down smile

Daffy Definitions

Garage .... What usually comes with a house attached.

Gossip .... What happens when we let the chat out of the bag.

Grandparents ..... People who adore your children, but who are certain you're not raising them right.

Hair .... Guaranteed to prevent baldness.

Lamb .... An animal that gets more sheepish every year.

Moon .... A perpetual nightlight.

Mosquito .... A buzzing insect that makes flies look good.

Raisin .... A very worried looking grape.

Salt .... It's useful in a pinch.

Secret .... A bit of news we tell to one person at a time, and in private.

Show-off .... Anyone more talented and energetic than ourselves.

Daffy Definitions

Sleep .... A fleeting moment that ends alarmingly.

Stress .... What happens when you wake up screaming, only to realize you haven't fallen asleep yet.

T .... The difference between here and there.

Tact .... Changing the subject without changing your mind.

Teenager .... One whose hang-ups don't include clothes.

Vacuum cleaner ...... Broom with a roar and a stomach.

Waffle .... A pancake with a nonskid surface.

Weeds .... Plants whose beauty has yet to be publicized.

Worry .... Interest paid on trouble before it falls due.

Wrinkles .... What others have; we have laugh lines.

Yesterday .... The tomorrow that got away.

Zoo .... Where animals observe funny-looking people.

Our Four-Legged Friends

Just as two fleas were walking out of a theater, it started to rain hard. "Shall we run for it?" asked one flea.

"No, we'd better take a dog," said the other.

●

Dogs will come when you call. A cat, however, will take a message and get back to you later. Maybe.

●

A young boy looked through the backyard fence and saw his neighbor with her large Newfoundland dog. "I'll bet he eats a lot!" said the boy. "Where does he get his food from?"

"From the supermarket," his neighbor replied.

"Really?" said the boy. "Do you drive him?"

Our Four-Legged Friends
Good Question

A baby camel turned to his mother and asked, "Mom, why was I born with a hump on my back?"

"Because you're a camel," Mom said, "and your hump holds food and water to help you travel for long distances through barren deserts."

"I see," said the baby camel. "Then how come I have such long eyelashes?"

Mom replied, "That's to protect your eyes from the grit and sand blown around by strong desert winds."

"Neat. Why do I have such big padded feet?" the baby camel continued.

"That's so we can walk through soft desert sand without sinking," explained his patient mom.

"Then what am I doing standing around in a Minneapolis zoo?"

Words from Wise Guys

*Cheerfulness keeps up a kind of daylight
in the mind, and fills it with a steady
and perpetual serenity.*

Joseph Addison

*There is no duty we so much underrate
as the duty of being happy.*

Robert Louis Stevenson

*If you would rule the world quietly,
you must keep it amused.*

Ralph Waldo Emerson

Humor is mankind's greatest blessing.

Mark Twain

*It is requisite for the relaxation of the mind that we
make use, from time to time,
of playful deeds and jokes.*

Thomas Aquinas

Q&A Time

Q: How come it's impossible to fool a snake?
A: Because you can't pull its leg!

Q: What did the hat say to the tie?
A: You hang around while I go on ahead.

Q: What's farther away, the moon or the North Pole?
A: The North Pole, of course. You can see the moon.

Q: Every wonder where the sun goes after it sets?
A: The answer will dawn on you.

LOL!

Anyone who says...

- It's a small world has never tried to paint it.
- That a penny saved is a penny earned hasn't looked at the price of groceries lately.
- He can't stand the heat hasn't got a swimming pool.
- Money can't buy happiness doesn't know where to shop.
- You can have everything in life obviously thinks you own multiple storage units.
- He has a perfectly clear conscience most likely has a perfectly poor memory.
- Teamwork is important likes to have someone around to blame.
- She can laugh at herself will always have something to laugh at.
- He's confident he can solve the problem doesn't yet understand the problem.

Very Punny!

A piece of string asked the barista for a latte. "I'm afraid I can't serve a piece of string," the woman said. So the string went outside, frizzed his hair, and returned to the barista. She eyed him suspiciously. "Aren't you the same piece of string I saw a few minutes ago?"

"No," replied the string, "I'm a frayed knot."

•

A man doubled over with back pain was advised by his doctor to see a chiropractor, but he didn't believe a chiropractor could do him any good. He went anyway, and after a few minutes' treatment, the man could stand straight up, completely pain free. When he went back to his doctor, the doctor said, "So how do you feel about chiropractors now?"

"I stand corrected," the man said.

LOL!

Did you hear the one about...

- The guy who bought a big-screen TV? Unfortunately, he didn't have the remotest idea how to turn it on.
- The woman who was told that a camera makes her look ten pounds heavier? From that day on, she stopped eating cameras.
- The gal who got a call from her bank? Seems her reality check bounced.
- The office intern who was determined to push the envelope? Try as he might, however, the envelope remained stationery.
- The barista who quit her job? She got tired of the daily grind.
- The gal who always laughed last? It took her a long time to get the joke.

Calorie Count

A balanced diet is having a chocolate chip cookie in each hand.

She went off her diet when she discovered that cottage cheese makes awful hot fudge sundaes.

Minutes at the table don't add weight—it's the seconds.

It's high time to get on a diet when you can pinch an inch—on your forehead.

Hear the one about the fellow who stepped onto a talking scales? After a few wheezes and whirs, the scales said, "Only one person on the scale at a time, please."

If you cheat on your diet, you'll gain in the end.

She had no problem going on a diet, except when she was hungry.

So true: More diets start in front of department store mirrors than on the scales at the doctor's office.

Life's Lessons

I learned that...

- The shirt I'm wearing stains easily: I fed a baby.
- The quickest way to learn if planes are taking off right on time is to arrive at the gate three minutes late.
- Not getting what I want is sometimes the best thing that can happen to me.
- Actions don't always speak louder than words. Ever watched a mime perform?
- The most becoming thing I can wear is a smile.
- If it weren't for the last minute, I'd never get anything done.
- When everything's coming my way, I'm probably in the wrong lane.
- The words I used yesterday weren't very sweet: Today I had to eat them.
- The quickest way to find out if a misplaced cell phone is gone for good is to buy a new one.
- Being kind is more important than being right.
- It's okay to make mistakes, because only mediocre people are at their best all the time.

Q&A Time

Q: *What do you get when you cross poison ivy with a four-leaf clover?*
A: *A rash of good luck.*

Q: *Why couldn't the bicycle stand on its own?*
A: *Because it was too tired.*

Q: *What did the octopus like least about being an octopus?*
A: *Washing his hands.*

Q: *Why are cowboys' hats turned up on the sides?*
A: *So three of them can fit in a pickup.*

Getting Along…or Not!

Lesson Learned

Toward the end of summer, an educator injured his spine and returned to school wearing a plaster cast around his upper back and chest. Under his shirt, the cast wasn't visible at all.

The first few days of school proved trying, as his students were noisy, cocky, and disrespectful. When he had had enough, he walked to the window of the classroom, opened it, and sat down again. In a few minutes, the breeze made his tie flutter. He picked up his stapler and stapled his tie to his chest.

From that moment through the end of the year, he presided over a class of model students.

Words from Wise Guys

We are all here for a spell;
get all the good laughs you can.

Will Rogers

It is pleasing to the dear God whenever you rejoice or
laugh from the bottom of your heart.

Martin Luther

You discover more about a person in an hour of play
than in a year of conversation.

Plato

Good humor may be said to be one of the very best
articles of dress one can wear in society.

William Makepeace Thackeray

The best doctors in the world are Doctor Diet,
Doctor Quiet, and Doctor Merryman.

Jonathan Swift

Time to Eat!

Q: *What did the little plate say to the big plate?*
A: *Lunch is on me.*

Q: *Why should you never tell a joke to an egg?*
A: *Because you'll crack it up!*

Q: *Why couldn't the coffee bean go out on Friday night?*
A: *Because he was grounded.*

Q: *Waiter, is there any soup on the menu?*
A: *Used to be, but I wiped it off.*

Q: *Why was the corn the most popular vegetable in the garden?*
A: *Because he was always willing to lend an ear.*

So True!

You're only young once, but immaturity can last a lifetime.

Small towns are great places to live, because if you don't know what you're doing, someone else will tell you.

Never tell a lie to an X-ray technician! She can see right through you.

A bird in the hand makes blowing your nose extremely difficult.

The only thing you can get free of charge these days is a dead battery.

Life not only begins at 40, but it begins to show.

Always go the extra mile, especially when what you want is a mile away.

Our Four-Legged Friends

How Much Is That Doggy in the Window?

A woman passes a pet store and sees a sign that says "Talking Dog for Sale." Intrigued, she goes in and asks the manager about the dog.

The pooch hears and pipes up: "Ever since I've been a pup, I've worked for the CIA, going to top-level meetings, hearing what's being said, and reporting back to headquarters. After a few years doing that, I joined the FBI. I could get into places other agents couldn't, and I was instrumental in the capture of a dozen most-wanted criminals in the nation."

Clearly impressed, the woman asks the manager how much he wants for the amazing dog.

"Ten dollars," he says.

"Ten dollars!" she exclaims. "Why would you let a dog with such remarkable talent go for only ten dollars?"

"Because he's a liar," the owner says. "He hasn't done any of those things."

LOL!

Did you hear the one about...

- The cowboy dressed in a paper shirt, paper jeans, paper jacket, and paper hat? He was arrested for rustling.
- The two geologists looking at a fissure in a rock? One says to the other, "Not my fault."
- The gal who went to dinner with a chess champ? It took him twenty minutes to pass the salt.
- The guy who swallowed a spoon? After that, he tried really hard not to stir.
- The bald guy who received a comb for his birthday? He promised he'd never part with it.
- The invention that lets you see through walls? It's called a window.
- The trainee pilot who flew through a rainbow? He passed with flying colors!

If Something Can Go Wrong...

Help!

A man was preparing to jump out of a plane for the first time. "Now if the pull cord doesn't work," his instructor reminded him, "just pull the backup cord, okay?"

"Okay!" the man said confidently, and with that, he jumped. After ten seconds, he pulled the first cord. Nothing happened. Concerned, he pulled the backup cord, but again, the 'chute didn't open. Now he panicked.

Just as he was frantically thinking what to do, a woman suddenly shot past him into the sky. "Hey, lady!" he yelled, "you know anything about parachutes?"

"No," she yelled. "You happen to know anything about gas stoves?"

LOL!

His wife went into labor and the man frantically dialed 911. When the dispatcher answered, he cried, "My wife is about to have a baby! What do I do?"

"Calm down, sir" the dispatcher said. "Now, is this her first baby?"

"No! This is her husband!" the man screamed.

•

A woman was hosting an outdoor luncheon for her friends. At the same time, two gardeners were working in the yard next door. Suddenly one of the gardeners jumped into the air, spun around, and leaped across the grass. The entire luncheon party turned and watched.

"What an impressive dancer!" exclaimed one of the guests. "Do you suppose that young man would come and entertain at my next party?"

When the host asked the other gardener, he called out, "Say, Ed, you think you could step on that ant's nest again at this other lady's house?"

Glass Half Full

You know you're an optimist if...

- You believe that things are the best that they can be.
- When you go fishing, you bring along your camera, a jar of tartar sauce, and a frying pan.
- You see an opportunity in every problem.
- You believe that if anything bad is going to happen, it will be postponed.
- You feel good when you feel bad, because you know you'll feel better tomorrow.
- You talk about the good things you have.
- You expect the best, and you're right.

Glass Half Empty

You know you're a pessimist if...

- You're afraid that things are the best that they can be.
- When you go fishing, you bring along a few fish burgers from a fast-food chain.
- Your see a problem in every opportunity.
- You believe that if anything bad is going to happen, it will.
- You feel bad when you feel good for fear you'll feel worse tomorrow.
- You talk about the bad things that could happen.
- You expect the worst, and you're right.

LOL!

A kindergarten class was on an outing to the local police station. As an officer was showing them around the department, one kid spotted a bulletin board with the pictures of the ten most-wanted criminals. He raised his hand and asked the officer if those were real photos of the bad guys.

"Yes, they are, son," the officer replied.

"Well," responded the boy, "why didn't you just handcuff 'em after you took their pictures?"

•

At the bank, a woman stood in line about ten minutes before it was her turn at the teller's counter. "I'm sorry about your wait, ma'am," the teller said.

Taken aback, the woman replied indignantly, "Well I declare, you're not exactly Miss Skinny yourself!"

Mind Your Manners!

Mama rabbit scolded her inquisitive little bunny by saying, "a magician pulled you out of a hat, that's how! Now stop asking so many questions!"

●

A robot said to the pump at the gas station, "It's rude to stick your finger in your ear when I'm talking to you!"

●

The boy octopus shyly approached the girl octopus and asked, "May I hold your hand, hand, hand, hand, hand, hand, hand, hand?"

Ha, ha, ha!

Laughter is like...

- Manure. It's no good unless you spread it around.
- A passport. It will take you where you want to go.
- Good medicine, only with no bad side effects.
- Changing the baby's diaper. It makes things more pleasant for a while.
- A light bulb. It lets people know someone's at home.
- A stick. You can even break ice with it.
- A fountain of youth. It takes ten years off your age.
- A souvenir. It reminds you of happy times.
- Music. It soothes the senses and uplifts the heart.
- Sunshine. It makes you feel really, really good all over!

Humor is the great thing,
the saving thing, after all.
The minute it crops up,
all our hardnesses yield,
all our irritations and
resentments flit away,
and a sunny spirit
takes their place.

Mark Twain